All Night

All Night

Grass Roots Press

First published in 2013 by Grass Roots Press

Grass Roots Press gratefully acknowledges the financial support for its publishing programs provided by the following agencies: the Government of Canada through the Canada Book Fund and the Government of Alberta through the Alberta Foundation for the Arts.　Alberta Foundation for the Arts

Grass Roots Press would also like to thank ABC Life Literacy Canada for their support. Good Reads® is used under licence from ABC Life Literacy Canada.

Library and Archives Canada Cataloguing in Publication

Cumyn, Alan, 1960-, author
　　All night / Alan Cumyn.

(Good reads)
ISBN 978-1-77153-001-9 (pbk.)

　　1. Readers for new literates.　I. Title.　II. Series: Good reads series (Edmonton, Alta.)

PS8555.U489A55 2013　　　428.6'2　　　C2013-902652-5

Printed and bound in Canada.

For Gwen and Anna, and their young men

Chapter One

The night is so cold as we run down the dark alley. I will never, never, never again take a bus to a funeral. A funeral that's out of town.

"Open the door!" Jess says behind me.

I drop the key in the slush by my feet. Why didn't I bring gloves? My fingers are freezing.

I wipe the slush off the key, jab it at the lock. "Come on!" I mutter.

"Gregor. Damn it!" Jess says.

She is tiny and very beautiful in her prom dress, with her pink ski jacket on top. Even in the dark. Even this late at night.

I bend down to try to see the keyhole clearly. The key finally slides in. The lock is so loose I have to hold it with my other hand as I turn the key.

When the door is open we race down the stairs. I slap on the overhead light. There it is: our one room. One room for almost everything: the old fridge, the pullout couch, the hot plate. No oven. And no kitchen sink. We wash dishes in the bathroom.

"God, I hate that light," Jess says. She slaps it off, as if the ugly, glaring light were my fault. Then she turns on the light by our bed, the pullout couch.

We just need to go to sleep, I think.

"It's so cold in here!" Jess says. We take off our jackets anyway. I stand in front of the fridge and look in. I can't help it. I'm hungry.

"We are never taking a bus to a funeral again!" she says. My feelings exactly. She pulls out the bed. I get out the milk and reach for the cereal box. Not much left. I empty the last of the cereal into a bowl.

"You have to get your driver's licence," I say. "Then we'll be able to rent a car the next time we need to go out of town."

Just as I'm about to pour the milk, she says, "That cereal is all we have for breakfast."

I stop. "Really?" I say. "You waited till I was about to pour." Then I think: why did I say that? I don't want to start an argument. I just want to go to bed.

I just want to hold her in bed.

"I did not wait," she says. "I just couldn't believe you would eat all of our breakfast."

The wrong word now and we could be up all night fighting. Not that we fight, not often. But losing our friend Peter and then going to his funeral has been hard.

"Why do I have to get my driver's licence?" she says. I return the milk to the fridge. I eat one flake, then I pour the rest of the cereal back into the box. Dust and all.

She's hurt, she wants to fight, and I have to be careful. I have to stick with a safe topic. So I say, "You came the closest to getting your licence. If only that stupid car hadn't stopped in front of you when you were taking your test. We could be renting by now." It was a small accident. She needs to try again.

She needs to believe enough in herself to keep going.

I turn on my old laptop. It used to be Peter's. It was too slow even for him. But it works.

"We have no money to rent a car," Jess says. "That's the big problem. You aren't checking messages now, are you?"

The laptop takes forever, but finally my e-mail comes up. The conference centre needs me tomorrow, first thing. Before first thing!

"I have to set up chairs for a big meeting in the State Room at eleven o'clock in the morning," I say. "I have to be there at nine-thirty. That room is huge. You could park a train in it and no one would notice."

"How many chairs will you have to move?" she asks.

"I don't know. Hundreds. Hundreds of thousands."

"So you might build some muscles or something?" It's the first nearly funny thing she has said since the bus.

Why is this computer so slow? There are other messages ... The Rats' Nest, a comedy club, wants my team to perform on Saturday night.

"Hey," I say, and glance at Jess, about to tell her the good news. She is lying on top of the bed in the blue silk slip she had on under her prom dress.

The one I got her from the second-hand store last Christmas.

She's so hot she could melt butter in that slip.

"Wait a minute," I say. "Are you—?"

But she gets up quickly and changes into her flannel pajamas.

"Wait a minute," I say again. "Was that—?"

She hops deep under the covers. "Too late. I'm freezing."

I push the laptop aside and hurry to the bed. But I don't get in, not yet.

"Too late!" she says. "You saw it. You blinked."

I start to rub her back. She closes her eyes and makes purring noises, in her way. I let my tuxedo jacket fall from my back and onto the floor. How silly to wear a formal costume like that to a funeral. And the suit isn't even mine, it belonged to Jess's father. I kiss her neck.

"Too late," she says.

I pull off the bow tie and undo my fancy shirt.

"You could just do my..." she murmurs.

I reach under the blankets and rub her bum.

"Mmm..." she says.

I worm my way out of my suit pants and socks. Then I slip under the blankets beside her.

"You're not going to leave my dad's clothes on the floor," she says. A whisper. With an edge.

"They all have to be dry cleaned anyway," I say.

I kiss her neck again. Why are my lips still cold? Because I'm so skinny. I lose heat easily.

But she has stopped purring. Right. All the clothes had been her father's. I groan but get out of bed anyway and pick them up. I race across the freezing room and hang the tuxedo in the closet.

"We could not have been more stupid," she says. "Dressing up like that for Peter's funeral."

"Well, everyone knows Peter and I have... *had*... a comedy act," I say.

"But they didn't get the joke, did they?"

Suddenly the door blows open and lets in a blast of icy air. Is the lock broken now? I dash up the stairs, slam the door shut, and stare at it, as if that might keep it closed. Then I dash back into bed and run with my legs to warm up the sheets.

"Did you break the lock?" Jess asks. She wants to fight. She wants to fight. Why is she in such a mood?

Because of Peter. Maybe we need to talk about Peter. So I say, "How could he just wake up dead like that?"

"Are you trying to be funny?" Jess says.

"I'm sorry," I say. I stop running and reach for her. She is warm already, and soft, and good to hold.

"He isn't going to wake up." She turns off the light.

We breathe together. I think about what I almost asked her on the bus. But timing is everything. Better to stay quiet now. Go to sleep. I just need to ... nuzzle closer. But she keeps an inch between us. The cold has crept into the blankets.

"He was only twenty-eight," she says. "A few years older than us. I've never had a friend just, like, die before. He had a nice body. How could he—?"

Sleep, sleep. How can she not be bone tired? Because she slept on the bus. I move my thigh against hers. That's all I want now.

She has the sweetest voice. A man could ... could get lost in a voice like hers ..."Hey!" She elbows me, not hard, just hard enough. "I can't believe you're asleep already! I was talking about Peter."

"I heard you," I sputter. It's dark here in the cold. I don't really want to open my eyes.

"What did I say?"

"You said he had a nice body."

"What else?"

"And that you were lusting after him," I joke, "and now that he's dead ..."

"Shut up!" she says. She pulls the blankets around her body. My feet stick out in the night. Now I really am awake.

Jess is winding me up. So I say, "You wondered how a guy who can sing 'O Canada' in Pig Latin can just have his heart stop in the middle of the night. And he wasn't even, you know, with anybody."

"There was no nooky," Jess says.

"No necking, no nibbling ..." I try to nibble her neck.

"Stop it!" She turns her head away but I follow. I kiss her hair, her shoulder. Search for her mouth. She pushes my arm, and my hand ends up around her small wrist. But she tears free and slaps me. God!

Hard. Right on the face.

I can see her in the light coming in from the alley through our one tiny window. She looks startled, as if she can't believe what she has just done.

"Ow!" I say, rather late, and sit back holding my jaw, stunned.

Chapter Two

"Sorry." Jess's voice is thin, and she looks down at the blankets, not at me. She has never hit me before, and I have never hit her. I never would.

She must be twisted up about Peter.

"I'm not in the mood," she says.

"Okay." I would have been happy with just a kiss.

"I didn't, like, use a lot of power," she says. Joking now, sort of. A good thing she didn't plow me. She is not very big, but her father was a fighter, and he trained her. He made his living by keeping the books at a tai chi studio. He took in all the money from students for lessons, and he paid the bills. But tai chi was his real passion. He loved how peaceful the slow movements made him feel. Just like all the martial arts, though, tai chi is also about fighting. Jess is no tai chi expert, but she is strong and fast. She might have broken my nose or something.

"It's all right," I say. "I wasn't trying to force you or anything. I'm sorry if I made you think that."

"No teeth loose?" She kisses me now. Lightly. "I just don't think we should make love tonight."

"No," I say. "Of course not." I lie back down. I could try to hold her again but I turn my back instead. I just stay quiet.

"We need to think about Peter," she says. "We have to honour him. His death has to change things for us, doesn't it? Life is showing us something here. Everything we know could be pulled out from under us. It's a wake-up call."

I press my cheek into the pillow.

"I don't think we should go to sleep tonight," Jess says. "You have to get up early anyway. What's the point? We should stay up and really talk about things."

She turns on the light.

"You mean about Peter?" I ask finally.

"About life! What we want from it. What we're doing here. Where we're going. How we feel! You start."

My face still stings from her slap. The words spill out of me. "Okay. How I feel: I'm starving. But I don't want to ruin my breakfast. So I'm here with you. My beautiful girlfriend. Tired but not sleeping. A bit beaten up. And we're not making love. You're in your mother's pajamas anyway. Some things a man can overcome..."

"Is that it?" she says.

"Pretty well."

"Okay," she says. She rolls over.

We are on a wire high above a black pit. I know this. I know. But the words keep tumbling out. "What happened to staying up all night? To honouring Peter with our blazing honesty?"

She does not open her eyes. "Just go to sleep. Dream about Karla." She seems to harden in front of me, becomes as still as glass.

"What do you mean, 'Dream about Karla?'"

"You know what I mean."

I shake my head slowly. "I talked to many people tonight, not just Karla. I didn't eat enough, so now I'm starving. Why do we never have any food in this house?"

Jess leaps out of bed. She pulls a blanket to the small, sagging chair in the corner and sits very still. "This is not a house. And we don't have any food because it's eighteen blocks to the grocery store. You don't help, so I just buy what I can carry. And what we can afford, which is not a lot. And you talked to Karla for half an hour. Which I don't mind at all. I mind the way you were looking at her."

This apartment is freezing. Of course I help with the shopping. Sometimes.

I pull the rest of the blankets around me. All right. The fight has started. But, I think, one problem at a time. I say, "How was I looking at her?"

She makes a funny, love-struck face.

I say, "I don't even know how to do that with my face. I have no idea what you're talking about."

"You used to look at me like that," she says.

I can't help it, I blow out until my lips flap. "All right. Hold on. It's late, we're both worn out. We will never, ever, take a bus out of town to a funeral again. Or dress up for one in costumes. I forgive you, you forgive me. Forget about staying up. Erase everything. Come to bed and go to sleep." I turn out the light. "Good night!"

Jess does not move. "Wow. Now I'm more worried than ever about Karla."

I toss and turn in the bed. "Oh, for God's sake! Why are you doing this?"

She does not move.

"Stop looking at me!" I cry.

She keeps staring.

"This whole thing hit Karla hard," I say. "She needed to talk to somebody. You know we used to go to school together."

Jess pulls at her hair. "She and Peter broke up two years ago. She's had eight boyfriends since. She just wanted to see how beautiful she would look in black. And you were there like some white knight."

I slump into the pillow. "Jess..."

"She's gorgeous! She's needy! She collects men like prize ribbons and then throws them away."

I can't stand it. I drag my own blankets out of bed and kneel beside her. "I am not anybody's prize ribbon!"

"Well, I should hope not."

I hold both her hands. Hers are chilly now, mine warm. "I don't think we're honouring Peter by fighting over Karla. She means nothing to me. She's *my* ribbon. Here, I'm pulling her off and throwing her away. Be gone!" I pretend to pull a ribbon off my chest and wave my arms to make it disappear in the shadows.

"You really are a goof." At last, a hint of a smile from her. "What are you doing?"

"I'm giving you my love-struck look." I lean in for a kiss. I am owed at least one.

She nudges my shoulder. "Shut up!" But she giggles, too, at last. We kiss slowly. Warm lips now, as well. We both have warm lips. Finally.

But then she pulls away.

"My turn," she says.

Chapter Three

Jess pauses. A look in her eyes. She has been thinking about what she wants to say for a long time. Maybe all the time I thought she was asleep on the bus. Or longer.

"I feel as if there's never enough money," she says. "Not for food, not for clothes. Not for good makeup. Or an actual hair style. There isn't enough money for a decent place to live. Think of it: natural light from proper windows! A garden with a rose bush!"

I reach for her hand again but she clenches her fist.

"I'm an actor, but I can't afford voice classes," she says. "But that's not the real problem. The real problem is, there's never going to be enough money. You have a part-time job stacking chairs.

I'm just a restaurant hostess. It's hourly wage crap. I could put up with being poor if we were getting somewhere. But we're not. You do comedy for no pay. After three years of theatre school, the only acting work I get is being an extra in crowd scenes. Peter was just like us, spinning his wheels. Now he's dead. I don't want that to happen to me."

I wait a moment for her to calm down. "You've already had voice classes," I say.

Jess throws up her hands. "I need more! I need acting for the camera. I need stage movement. I'm years away from being really good. And to get there, I need help. To get help, I need money."

I try to hold her again. It was warmer, much warmer in bed. "You're a lot better than you know. When you perform in a show, I can't keep my eyes off you. And I'm not the only one."

She pushes me away. "You're just thinking about after the show." She takes all the blankets with her and settles back into bed. I am alone out here in the cold in my T-shirt and boxer shorts.

"I didn't tell you about the other e-mail I got," I say. "My comedy team is on for Saturday at the Rats' Nest."

"The Rats' Nest?"

I squirm into bed beside her again. "It's a really cool new place. Very hip. Everyone wants to play at the Rats' Nest now. But we won't have Peter on the team, of course."

"Because Peter is dead. Will they pay you?"

I pause. "A beer each."

"You wouldn't want to miss that," she says. "Just because your partner and friend is dead. You know what this reminds me of? The elephants!"

"Not the elephants," I moan. A year ago we watched a special on elephants on National Geographic TV. Since then the elephant story has showed up in every argument we have had.

Jess begins to shuffle around the room. She swings her arms together like a trunk. "There they are, the mothers. And the little orphan elephant is trapped in the mud hole."

"Shut up!" I say. But of course I watch her. Performing, she has an extra glow.

"All the female elephants pull that orphan out and adopt him! But what are the males doing? They're off at the water hole, the big bulls. And poor Grampa elephant is trying to get in, to take a sip. But they won't let him! He's old and weak. He stands in the heat for hours until—"

Jess falls back on the bed. She twitches, lies still. Then she gets up. "And all the bulls run around Grampa. They trumpet: what a great elephant he used to be! But did they lift a trunk to save him?"

I pull her under the covers again. "Enough of you and your elephants," I say. "I sat on a bus for hours in the cold in the wrong clothes to mourn my friend. Doing our act at the Rats' Nest is another way of honouring him. And besides, people from the Second City club might be there. You never know who will hire us next."

"To pay you what?" Jess asks. "French fries?"

I rub my empty belly. "French fries would be good right now. I would kill to get a basket of french fries right now."

She rubs my skinny belly, too. Warm, warm hand. "Let's not kill anybody, okay?"

"It's just a figure of speech," I say.

Something flits across the floor. Jess sits up. "Oh damn! I saw one! I saw one!" She squirms on the bed. I peer into the gloom. "Do you see it?" she asks. "Do you see it?"

There it is—a cockroach! I grab a shoe and hammer along the floor. There and…there! I chase it, hammering.

"Is it dead?"

I blow roach guts off the shoe. "You wouldn't happen to have any french fries, would you?"

When I get back to bed Jess holds me close. "My hero! I'm sorry, I'm sorry. I'm just...I shouldn't have talked you into wearing that tuxedo. Over-dressing was stupid. I don't know what I was thinking."

"You were thinking of your father," I say. "His tux is just a little big on me."

"We should have shown more respect. Now Peter's family thinks we're just clowns or something. As if we thought it was Halloween."

I stroke her hair. It's going to be all right. "Peter loved Halloween. And Peter loved you. He really did."

"I know," she says.

"He wasn't just carrying a torch for you. His torch was like a...a flame-thrower!"

Why did I say that? She shakes my hand away. "Shut up."

I have started, so I keep going. "If he hadn't died, he would have been all over you. He was just waiting for me to exit the scene."

"He was not."

So much for talking truths! I should just shut up. And yet I can't. "He tried to kiss you that night at the thing," I say. "At that swimming party."

"He was drunk."

"Peter was never really drunk in his whole life. As soon as he saw you, he knew what he wanted."

Jess pulls a pillow over her head. "Can't we just go to sleep?"

So that's the way it is! I move closer. "What, and not honour Peter? It was your idea. You're the one who wanted to talk about things."

"Important things. The changes we need to make."

"What changes? We are on a path. I need to do my act at the Rats' Nest because the Second City club might be next. You need to check your messages. A gig might have come up for you."

She hits me with a pillow. Feeble, a glancing blow. "Nothing has come up for me."

"I know I joke around a lot," I say, "but this I truly believe: the world can change in a day. Are you ready for it? That's the big question here."

"I'm *not* ready for it," Jess says. "I need more voice classes. We're out of money. I can't even afford to get my picture taken. A proper head shot. By a real photographer. How are we going to have kids?"

Kids? Is that what our fight is about? "We'll, um, raise them in a shoe box, to start," I say. "We'll get deals at the Goodwill store. We can pay for everything they need on credit and then get new cards."

"Very funny," she says. "You're just a scream."

But I'm not laughing. Can't she see that? "Do you really want a guy in a suit who rents his soul to some company?"

"If his sperm is good and he can pay the bills."

What? Why is she saying such things? "Maybe ten years from now we might be ready for kids. What's the rush? I thought you didn't want to be hemmed in."

Jess gets up and begins pacing. She has heavy feet for someone so small. "I feel trapped and poor. I don't feel as if I have ten years to spend on a risky career. We just got the warning shot. Go to sleep tonight, tomorrow might not happen."

She shivers, even in her mother's thick pajamas. "It's freezing in here!" she cries.

She picks up the phone.

"You are not calling our landlord," I say.

"You're right," Jess replies. "I'm not. You are! Tell him he might find two blue corpses first thing in the morning."

She carries the phone to me in bed. It's the middle of the bloody night.

"I'm not calling!"

"No, you're not calling," she says. "And you're not getting a good job. You're waiting for me. You want me to get some office job that will pay for you…"

"No."

She's still waving the phone at me. "We have to do something!"

"Start by checking your e-mail," I say. "Some film director might be looking for you!"

She punches in our landlord's number and holds the phone out for me.

"I'm not taking it!" I fall out of bed trying to get away.

"Yes you are!" Are we doing this? I scramble in the cold, she chases me with the phone. We go around and over the bed. She grabs my leg and pins me down. I hate wrestling with her. She's tiny and too good! And if, somehow, I win, she pretends to be just a girl, anyway.

On my back, on the floor, I finally take the phone. "It's the machine," I say.

"Well, leave a message!" Her hair is falling in my face. I could just sort of help her move towards me. I think of her at the reception in her dress, on the bus with her eyes closed.

Even when we are pulling apart, I feel as if we are moving together.

On the phone I say, "Hello, Mr. Stewart. It's, ah, Gregor Luft." I change my voice because Jess is listening. "We're, ah, close to the North Pole now, sir. But the weather is closing in. Jess has left me here. She's making a dash for it. I'm worried about her gear." I hold the phone away for a moment and make wind noises. "Not sure how much longer we can hold out here without heat, Mr. Stewart. Please call our families if you get this message. You might find us dead in the morning."

Jess grabs the phone. "Mr. Stewart, Gregor is just kidding. Well, not really. It is freezing in here. The heater has died again. Please, fix it! Thank you." She hangs up and throws the phone down. "Nothing is serious for you," she says. "Everything is a big joke."

"That's not true," I say. Why can't she see what that was? Not a big joke, a bridge of jokes. A way to be in this world. A way across a cold, dark river.

Why can't she see what I am about? Who I am?

"What are you doing Saturday night at the Rats' Nest?" she says. "To honour Peter? What's the plan?"

"It's improv comedy," I say. "We just say the first thing that comes into our heads. Even better if it's funny. There is no plan."

"So you and the third guy, what's-his-name, Jeremy. You haven't talked about how to honour your missing partner?"

"We haven't." The floor is cold. I move to get free of Jess but she pulls me back. I let her.

"You haven't actually replaced Peter already, have you? Mr. Elephant?"

I am not an elephant beside her. More a giraffe beside a herd dog.

"Of course we haven't replaced him yet."

"Can't you do improv with two people?"

"Not really, not as well," I say. "Three people are funnier. They can trip each other up. Aren't you cold?"

"No." She is focused. Focused on fixing me. "Okay," she says, "pretend it's Saturday night. Jeremy Elephant is away. It's just you. Some big talent agent is in the crowd. You're all alone onstage. What are you going to do?"

"I don't know," I say, and I mean it.

"Now, ladies and gentlemen! Direct from the filthy, frozen apartment he will never escape! Mr. Gregor Luft!"

I stay still.

"Master of stacking chairs and cleaning cake from carpets!"

"Shut up."

"Gregor Luft! The funniest man making minimum wage. It's your big moment."

"It's not my big moment. It's not Saturday night. I don't feel right." I pull free, get up, and see the hot plate. It's all we have for a stove, nearly useless for cooking. But that's not what we need right now. I turn it on. The hot plate element begins to glow orange.

I smile at Jess—she is looking at me. I hold my chilly hands over the hot plate burner. Surely she can see me now—the real me? The burner isn't much, but it's quietly funny, and a little warm. Lovely in the dark, like an old campfire. From back when we humans were hardly more than giraffes and elephants.

Any other time she would smile, but not tonight. Peter's death really has rattled her. "Let's just go to bed," she says, her voice now dim, like a candle flame almost out.

Chapter Four

Suddenly, the wind blows the door open again. I hadn't told the landlord a crazy story: we really are fighting arctic storms.

"Shut the door!" Jess wraps herself in blankets. "Come to bed!"

I jam a *National Geographic* magazine under the door to keep it closed. Then I return to my laptop.

"I hope there are no elephants in that magazine," Jess says. "If the lock is broken, how are we supposed to keep out burglars?"

"We have nothing to steal," I reply. "That will keep out burglars." On the laptop I try her account, but I can't get in. "Did you change your password?" I look up from the screen, waiting.

"Maybe."

"You never change your password."

"You haven't known me very long," she says. "I changed my password all the time before I met you."

My fingers are still waiting. "Two years is a long time. What's your new password?"

She tells me it's a secret because she doesn't know mine. But I *did* tell her, that night in the taxi, when we were stuck in the snow. She had decided she wanted to know everything about me.

I remind her of that conversation. "Oh, that famous night when we took a taxi!" she says. "We were just blowing through money!"

She's stalling. She really doesn't want me to know her password. Why would that be?

Because words have power. More than we know.

"I will tell you mine again," I say, "but then you might feel bad for not remembering, and blame me. So you need to forgive me now."

"I forgive you," she says.

"Okay. Here's the clue: one of the toilet inventors."

"Oh! Oh!" She holds her head in her hand. "A password so stupid I should never have forgotten it!"

"At least you forgave me," I say.

"But you must have changed it by now," she says.

"I don't go around changing things that are perfectly good," I reply.

"No. No one will guess 'Crapper.' Thomas, wasn't it?"

"Thomas Crapper. Now you tell me your password," I say.

Jess closes her eyes. "Can't you guess it? I thought you knew me better than that."

"You couldn't guess my password, and I'd already told you what it was!"

She sits up, not tired at all now. Ready to just keep on arguing. "But you're really smart. You could be doing a lot better than this. It's just about stacking chairs for you. Being in the moment. But you can't be in this moment. Where are you? Waiting for Saturday night, Mr. Elephant? That's the moment you want."

"What are you talking about?"

"If you knew me at all, you would know," she says.

I hold my head. "You're just ... just *looking* to make trouble."

"I am. I'm a troublemaker. I want someone who really, really knows me. Who pays attention. Who makes plans."

"I do make plans!" I say. "Didn't I buy the bus tickets with our credit card points from shopping at the grocery store? Tell me that didn't take planning. Saving and using those points."

"I do the shopping. You save the points. Some plan. But what's your plan about me, about our life together, about how we're going to pay the bloody bills? Now that we have no grocery points left?"

I press my lips together.

"You looked as if you wanted to say something," Jess says.

"I am sitting here, taking your criticism like a man. Not an elephant. Or a giraffe."

"Giraffe?" She softens. "Come to bed, Mr. Giraffe."

When I do get in bed, with the laptop, she touches my nose, a sudden, loving gesture. "Misty," she says.

I don't get it.

"That's my password!"

Misty. Misty... suddenly I hear Peter's voice in my head, talking to Jess. *"Misty, when are you going to dump this guy?*" The way he used to talk, even when I was around. Joking, but not really.

He loved her. He loved her. And she is using his pet name for her. She uses it for her password.

"Check my e-mail and let's go to sleep!" Jess says. She pulls the blankets over her head as if she doesn't care what might be waiting for her.

Chapter Five

Misty. Peter and Jess. Jess and Peter. Some things you have to put to one side. They will need thinking through. They can't be taken care of right away.

I type "Misty" on Jess's password line and then try to forget about it. "You have 2,081 unread messages," I say. "Don't you ever check your mail?"

She nudges me under the blankets.

"They are all junk messages, aimed at men with little thingies," she says. That wouldn't apply to Peter. He and I used to swim together. I don't want to think about his thingy.

"I knew it. I knew it!" I see the golden message she missed.

"What?"

"Ten o'clock. Tomorrow morning! An audition!"

"For what?" Jess pulls the blankets off her head. "What am I trying out for?"

"Sweeney Circle Acting School and Theatre."

"No!" She twists out of bed. Those small feet thumping on the floor. "I sent in my application months ago."

"And they replied last week. Why don't you read your e-mail? You have to be there at nine-thirty."

"I have nothing ready to perform!" she says.

"The acting school program lasts two years, and you get fully paid," I say. "The first year is training, and the second year you're in real plays with the other actors."

"But I have to try out! What am I going to do?" Jess wails. "I just . . . I could give them that speech I learned when I played the girl who joined the circus in that show. In *Whimsy.* But I haven't done it in ages. Do I even have the script anymore?"

She could do any number of things. I could give her a list. She could even do the elephants.

I read from the screen: "Actors are to perform three to five minutes of original work."

"Well, that sinks it," Jess says. She pulls at her hair as she walks around. She *can* do this. I know she can. But she says, "I don't do original work. I can't make things up. And there's no time now. Oh, forget it."

"You make things up all the time," I say. "What about the elephants?"

"The elephant story only works with you. You know everything I'm thinking. The acting judges at Sweeney Circle do not."

I do not know everything she is thinking. *Misty*, for example. *Peter*. But I get out of bed and catch her hands—colder than ever—to stop her pacing. "If you get this," I say, "we could rent a place on the planet's surface. With proper windows and natural light! Fresh air. A little...a little rose bush. You could smell it on your way to work in the theatre company of your dreams!"

"I can't make things up," Jess says. "I need a script."

But that is what I'm here for: I make things up all the time, even when I'm on stage. I clap my hands. "We'll just work out something right now. Okay? Pretend I'm a judge." I make my voice sound stern. "What is your name, dear?"

"Jess. Jess Hale."

"And what is your chosen topic for this morning, Ms. Hale?"

"Ah, you got me," Jess says.

I drop the phony voice. "No, that's not a good answer. What's in your head right now?"

"Death. My father's death."

"Excellent!" I become a judge again. "Please proceed."

Jess paces, paces. "Oh damn, oh damn! My father was ... a strange man."

"Don't tell me. Perform it!"

"My father was a fighter. He was a martial artist, a tai chi bookkeeper."

"Act it out!" I say. "Show me with your hands and arms." I punch the air.

"Shut up," Jess says. "This is not going to work."

"I have an idea. What were you doing—exactly— when you found out? About your father's death?"

"I've told you this, like, a hundred times," she says.

"I know. It's a good story. You could use it in the audition. Just be yourself. The judges will fall in love with you telling that story."

Like I did. I don't quite say it.

Jess shakes her arms loosely, moves her head from side to side to get ready to perform. "Well, I was sitting on a streetcar. And this guy who smelled of pee was standing in front of me. I felt sorry for him. I was ready to give him my seat. But the stink was like a wall I'd have to pass through."

"Great!" I jump on the bed. "Do the wall!"

"The wall?"

I hold my arms and hands flat, as if I am a wall.

Jess ignores me. "And my phone rings. It's my mom." She pretends to be on the phone. "'Hi, Mom. Can I call you back?'" Jess looks out at nothing, as if she might be on stage, with the lights shining in her face. The judges will love her. "I'm, like, how do I even breathe with this stench? The guy is looking at me. Does he want my seat? My phone? What?

"My mom says, 'No. Are you sitting?' She sounds tight. As if she can't breathe. 'Mom, are you all right?' She says, 'It's your father, dear.' And then a hole seemed to open up in the earth. I don't know how I got from the wall of stink and the streetcar to running along the street. Oh, God! The air felt like a thick liquid that I had to swim through. I was nearly home, but I felt as if I would never get there.

"I don't remember Mom saying, 'He's dead,' those exact words. She said, 'Daddy crumpled in the bathroom." Down he went. Standing at the sink, with the door open. He was clipping his nose hairs. And then he crumpled."

The Sweeney Circle judges will see and hear her like this and love her, love her like I do. But suddenly her face shuts. She says to me, "You're thinking I'll get in because the judges will feel sorry for me. That's sick."

"No. It's a good story. That's all. You've got this mighty martial arts bookkeeper father. And he crumples in the bathroom while clipping his nose hairs. That's life. That's life right there."

"Great," Jess says. "My father's nose hairs. A fine story."

"It needs an ending," I say.

"He died!" Jess says. "The end. I don't remember getting home. But when I got there, Mom had already dragged him into the bedroom. Somehow, she had lifted him onto the bed. She didn't want anyone to know that he died in the bathroom."

Just saying the words seems to split her open. In a moment she's crying. I hold her. She sobs into my shoulder. *Misty*. Peter's pet name for her. Because she does cry. A lot.

"That's not a story," she says. "It's the terrible thing that blew a hole in my family a couple of years ago. I'm not going to get picked."

"Shh," I say. She did cry today for Peter. She rained hard. We all did.

Jess says, "There are no lucky breaks. You don't get picked based on something you threw together a few hours before trying out."

"Sometimes it happens," I say. She has to believe that, if she wants to be an actor.

"Never. Not to me," she says.

I hold her so that she has to look into my eyes. "Tell them about later. With the moon and everything."

"It's hopeless," she says.

"How you were walking that night in the summer. And the moon was hanging like a huge, pregnant dinner plate in the sky."

Jess moves away. "A pregnant dinner plate?"

"I forget how you put it. How did you put it?"

She seems to have forgotten. But then she says, "The moon itself was like a beaming, pregnant belly. Like my father's belly. He was so proud of all the chi he packed into his insides. He said he was almost pregnant."

"They might not know what chi is," I say. "You could tell them it's healthy energy, sort of an Eastern idea."

Jess crosses her arms. Almost hugging herself. "Well, a fat lot of good Dad's healthy energy did him. His heart gave out. That could happen to anybody. How many more examples do we need?"

"But about that moon. Beaming down on you. And you had that feeling…"

"I guess."

"You were flooded with chi from the pregnant father moon," I say. She must remember telling me this. She must! "And a great weight lifted. Right? And then you just knew—"

"You remember," Jess says.

"Of course I remember! It was just about the first thing you said to me. Right after, 'Please pass the pickles.' You talked about your father, and the moon, and that feeling."

Her eyes light up first, and then her whole face, the way it does. Like when clouds move to show the sun. "We were at that party," she says.

"Yes! I passed you the pickles. And you said, 'Last night I was flooded with the feeling that everything is going to be all right.'"

"That's when we met," Jess says.

"You talked on and on. I almost asked you to marry me on the spot."

"You did not," she says quickly.

"I asked you to come with me to Peter's family's cottage the next weekend. Almost the same thing."

"Shut up," Jess says. But she is smiling. She is my Jess, no matter how late it is or what we might say to one another. I touch her cheek softly. "I loved you so much, right from that first pregnant moon story."

She brushes my hand away. "Yeah, so you say. But you didn't ask me to marry you. You have not asked me, you will not ask me. We are going nowhere." She moves away. "You are stacking chairs. And I am showing people to their tables. Wearing a low-cut blouse to get bigger tips."

"I am doing my comedy act at the Rats' Nest on Saturday night," I say slowly. "And you are auditioning for Sweeney Circle, which is two years at full pay." I breathe hard, as if climbing stairs. But there's no stopping now. "And I, Gregor Luft, am hereby asking you, Jess Hale . . ."

Her eyes widen.

". . . to marry me," I say.

45

Chapter Six

"Shut up," she says.

As if I am joking. As if I didn't mean every word of what I had just asked her.

Gently I hold her face in my hands. "Marry me."

"You're not even on one knee!"

I kneel down. "Jess Hale. Love of my life. Wounded daughter." My face is burning, as if the hot plate is right beside me. "Teller of the pregnant moon story. Wonderful actor. Future mother of our charming children. Marry me! Please!"

I wait, but she can't seem to look at me. *Whatever she means to say, it's not yes.*

Silence. All the air is gone.

"I'm going to ask you again." My voice cracks. "Will you please take this beating heart of mine out of my hands? Save my life. Marry me."

She looks to my left, not into my eyes. "You thought of this right now, didn't you?" she says. "You're just making it up. You have no ring. No plan. Twenty years from now, we're still going to be in this basement."

I swallow hard. "I do have a ring. I was going to ask you on the bus home. But then you slept most of the way. I think I picked the right time. I think this moment is exactly—"

"Don't lie to me!" she says.

My heart beats in my ears like a bass drum, but I stay quiet. Icy calm. "I'm not lying. Why do you say I'm lying?"

She sits on the edge of the bed, away from me. "That was such a strange weekend, the time we went to Peter's cottage."

"You're changing the subject."

"No, I'm not. You said you almost asked me to marry you when we first met. Instead, we went to Peter's cottage."

"He wasn't supposed to be there," I say.

"Gregor! You told me others would be there. Or I wouldn't have gone in the first place. I barely knew you!"

"Peter said he would stay for half an hour. Then he would go back to the city."

"That's how you planned it?"

"But he stuck around," I say. "He had fallen for you, too. As you and I both know. Remember when we were on the blanket, back in the shade, getting closer? Then Peter started yelling as if he was drowning? And you ran off to save him?"

"You wanted me to fall for *your* stupid plan, not his. You're just full of plans. But when you ask me to marry you, you don't even bring a ring. Do you know how that makes me feel?"

I don't move. "I have a ring. It's in the pocket of your father's tuxedo."

She steps towards the closet. As if she wants to prove me wrong. But then she stops. "Why don't *you* go get it?"

"I would," I say. My jaw is tight. "But you don't believe me. And I really, really need my future wife to trust my word. When I'm being serious. Like now."

"Go get it if you have it!" She is only a few steps from the closet herself.

I do not move. "That's not the issue right now."

Silence.

"I knew you didn't have it," Jess says. She throws herself back into bed and surrounds herself with pillows, as if for protection.

I'm hot and cold at the same time. I rush to the closet. There's the tux, but I don't touch it. I pull on my pants, my coat, my shoes. Up the stairs. The door won't open. I kick aside the magazine and then I am out. To hell with the door. She can close it behind me, she can ...

Down the alley. Running, running, in the slush and the wind. It's freaking cold. Why didn't I bring a hat?

I don't need one. I just run, run. Work my lungs, my legs. Feel the whole planet turning beneath my feet ...

She said *no*. I asked her to marry me. I showed her my soul, and she said ...

Well, she didn't say *no*, but she didn't say *yes*. So really, she said *no*.

Slap, slap, slap, my feet against the slushy road.

Where am I going?

I am just going.

To Peter's place. Of course. He'll know. He'll ...

Oh God, God, God, the truth hits me like an arm suddenly held out in the darkness. Where I'm going. What I'm doing. How my life is all coming apart.

Chapter Seven

I run around for a bit in the empty streets. I shout up at the moon, which does not answer. I watch my reflection in the black of shop windows. I should find a bar. Isn't that what men do?

But I do not find a bar, and I have no money, anyway. I circle around and around, and then I head back. Down the dark alley. To the closed door and past it, to our one window. I squat and look in. There she is, my Jess. Mine? I thought she was.

She is not mine. Just Jess. Standing in my... no, her father's... tuxedo, with her back to me. She must have checked in the pockets. What is she doing now? I can't hear what she's saying.

She looks as if she is pretending to talk to the acting school judges. Maybe about her father. About the nose hairs. Or how he would do tai chi fighting on the weekends for extra money. How he loved being in the ring. He'd fight anyone, a kick-boxer or maybe a karate guy. When he practised, his movements were very slow, but he was fast enough in the ring. She told me no one could knock him down.

But Jess is different. Her spirits do get low. I know that about her. She is a fighter, too, but she needs someone steady beside her.

Someone who doesn't take no for an answer. Or even *not yes*.

I find myself standing by the door, listening. Her voice is hard to hear, but I can just make out what she's saying.

"Ladies and gentlemen, let me tell you about Peter," she says. "Peter had these sideburns. *Has*. He has. Is he really gone? I don't believe it."

Quiet. I imagine Jess wiping her eyes. *Misty*. "These sideburns. He would shave them off and look so goofy, like a twelve-year-old. But they'd be back in a few days. You couldn't ... you couldn't keep him down. He would call in the middle of the night, blind drunk. He'd say, 'Jess. Jess, I love you?' Like a question. 'Where are you? What are you doing right now?' And I'd say, 'I'm sleeping. Beside Gregor, your friend. What do you want?'"

Her voice falls, and I strain to hear. "Peter told me, 'I want to just breathe the air you breathe. That's all. That's all I need.'" She gives a little laugh.

I am shaking, shaking in the cold. But I can't go in yet. She says, "I know Peter was drunk. But I would give anything, anything I've got, to hear that voice again: 'I want to just breathe the air you breathe.'"

I step away. I don't want to hear any more, so I walk back up the alley. But I really have nowhere else to go. When I turn around, I shuffle my feet as loudly as I can to warn her that I'm coming.

I hurry through the door and quickly shut it behind me. I jam the magazine in place. Jess is in bed now, in the dark, pretending to be asleep. The tuxedo jacket lies on the floor where she must have dropped it.

If she can pretend, so can I. "It's bloody cold out there!" I say. I pull off my outer clothes and jump into bed beside her.

"I've got freezer burn!" I say. I am a shivering ice cube beside her.

"Gregor," she says.

"Just don't say anything. Nothing! We've already said enough."

"You're shaking." She holds and rubs me.

"Not another word," I say. "Honestly. We have said way too much. All right?"

She stays quiet for a moment. Then she says, "I looked in the tux pocket."

Of course she did. And yet still she was thinking of Peter. *I just want to breathe the air you breathe.* He would say anything to impress her.

"Yes," I say. "You looked."

She turns on the light. "A toy snake jumped out of the box in the pocket and almost hit me in the eye. I screamed like you have never heard me scream."

"I'm sorry. I can explain everything," I say.

"I'd like to hear you try."

I sit up. "Did you check the other pocket?" When she doesn't move, I run from the bed and get the tuxedo jacket. From the pocket she did not look in, I pull out the small gift box she did not see.

Jess smiles grimly. "What's in there, a whoopee cushion?"

I just want to breathe the air you breathe. All right, Peter could be a poet. That's what she wants from me. I open the box: a beautiful old ring with tiny diamonds.

That's what she wants. I get down on one knee again.

"It was my grandmother's," I say. "I'm sorry. I was only going to use the snake if I had to."

"Why would you *ever* need to propose to your girlfriend with a toy snake?"

All right, my plan was silly, or worse. I was supposed to be there when she opened the box.

But I don't try to explain. I just say, "It was just in case we needed a laugh. After the funeral."

Jess still has not taken the ring. She must still be thinking about Peter. "So now," she says, "you're really proposing?"

What does she want to hear? "I can't think of how to live the rest of my life without you."

"Oh, Jesus."

"Please marry me."

"I'm too upset to think right now," Jess says.

"I'm not asking you to think." I tremble as I hold out the ring. Still on one knee.

"Get up," Jess says. "You're making me nervous."

I stay right where I am. "Marry me. Please."

Silence. She still can't look at me. *I just want to breathe the air you breathe.* That's what Peter would say. But I am not Peter.

I stand. Gregor Luft. Peter Beckwith is dead and gone. "Jess Hale. Marry me."

Jess says, "We just went to a funeral looking like clowns. How will we ever be adults?"

"What's so great about being an adult?" I reply. "Jess Hale. Please."

Peter is dead, and she didn't love him anyway. Not like she loves me. I know that. We used to laugh about Peter. She chose me, not him.

Slowly she gets out of bed, takes the ring and looks at it. It really is beautiful. "It was your grandmother's?" she says.

"She was married seventy-two years. Couldn't stop smiling."

Jess slips the ring onto her finger. But she still can't look me in the eye. "Aren't you supposed to kiss me?" she asks.

"You haven't said yes." I need her to say *yes*.

Jess fiddles with the ring. "If we were married for seventy-two years, then we'd be almost a hundred—"

"We will be happy dust together!" She needs someone who will not back down. "And we'll remember this day. This shining moment. Like seeing the pregnant dinner plate moon."

"Which I didn't remember until you reminded me," she says.

"But you will remember this. You will remember finding that snake—"

"Shut up."

"We'll say: 'We lived on cereal, then. When we had it. Breakfast cereal and love.'"

She takes the ring off and puts it on again, over and over.

"I need to hear you say yes," I say.

Finally she looks at me. But the words do not come. She firms her lips.

"You can't *not* say yes." My voice breaks. "Jess." Silence.

My knees buckle. I take a step backwards, to keep from falling over. "I can't believe this! Do you know how hard this is for me? You wear that ring, I won't stack chairs for more than another year at most. I won't look at another girl at a party, not even at a funeral. I won't work for beers anymore, never, never again! I have to build something that will be worthy, worthy of you and me, of this moment. Isn't that what you want to hear from me? Don't keep looking at me like that. You can't. Do you hear me? I want us to have everything together! All right?"

Quietly she takes off the ring.

"Jess?" My voice squeaks.

She puts the ring back in the box and closes the lid.

"Who are you?" she asks.

Chapter Eight

"What do you mean, who am I?" I cry. She really is making me crazy.

But she will not back down. "Where's the guy I've been living with for the past year?" she asks. "Is he just giving up?"

"Giving up?"

"Do you think I want some tamed guy? A guy who will hate me every time he looks at our one little rose bush?"

"I don't understand!"

"Do you think I want to crush your spirit? I don't want you to stop working for beers. I love that you work for beers!"

"But before you said—"

"Forget what I said! What kind of marriage do you want? One where we keep track of who said what, like keeping a ... a cricket score?"

"Cricket? Since when do you care about cricket?"

"Since never! All I know is, the score gets too high to count. And you shouldn't keep score, either!" She wraps me in her short, loving arms. Just like that, she looks as if she wants to be kissed.

"But what did we decide?" I ask.

We are both so tired we feel almost drunk. Silently, she gets back into bed. I snuggle in beside her. This is what I wanted. All along. Just to feel her. To hold her. "But what did we decide?" I ask once more.

The warmth, being warm again, feels so good. She presses her face against my chest. She says, "We will be interesting people. Together. All right?"

God, what a night! We must have said everything there is to say. And nothing else matters.

"All right," I say. The rest is just cricket scores.

She kisses me. *Oh.* Again and again. "Go to sleep," she says. "We are never doing this again."

"You couldn't pay me enough beers to ever do this again," I say.

"Shut up," Jess says.

We are warm, warm together.

"Even if you filled the fridge…"

Her body tenses into a yawn. "No more. Please. Just. Shut up."

She turns over and we snuggle even closer. Why couldn't we do this hours ago? Our bodies feel wrapped in the same heavy skin. In a minute she is snoring. *Snuffle-whiff, snuffle-whiff.* Gentle, gentle. I pull her even tighter.

She hugs the arm I lay over her. I bury my drowsy face into her hair.

Dreamless sleep. Drained of everything. Warm together.

Slowly, the light changes. I sense the change and I don't. Slowly, morning comes on.

Slowly, Jess wakes up. I see her in a dream, waking up. I am sleeping, but I see her somehow. Are my eyes open?

She sits up. "God! Gregor! Get it!"

I bolt awake. *"What?"*

"Get it! Get it! There!"

I twist out of bed and grab my shoe again. I hammer away, chasing the cockroach around and under the bed.

Jess screams, "It's over there now! Go!"

"I'm trying! I'm trying!" I shout.

"There! There! Oh, God, get it!"

I whack the roach. Whack! Whack! There—got it! Jess runs into my arms, knocking me to the floor. "My hero!"

Oh, we kiss as if we are gasping for air. Like we should have kissed all last night! Instead of fighting. I manage to pick her up, then dump her back on the bed. I dive on top of her.

"Wait," she says.

"What?"

"What time is it?"

"Really?" I groan. I scramble to find my watch. "It's 9:07"

"*What?*"

Oh God, oh...I spring out of bed. "It's 9:07! 9:07! It's seven minutes after bloody nine."

Jess madly starts pulling on clothes. "Oh God! Oh God!" she cries.

I shove our one bowl of cereal towards her. "Here! Here!"

She almost knocks it with her elbow. "But you have to stack all those chairs," she says. "You have it!"

We take turns eating cereal while trying to pull on clothes. She hurries into the black leggings she always wears when she tries out for a part. The long red top with the narrow sleeves.

"You have to go!" I say. "If you catch the subway—"

"I'll never make it!"

"You can! You can!" We've made it this far. We made it through last night.

"Oh God, I'm just going to make a fool of myself."

I help her into her winter coat. "You are stunning. You'll be great. I love you. Now go!"

"You have to go to work, too!"

"I'm coming!" I say. "I'm coming! Just go!"

I push her out the door. I finish the last of the cereal, spilling milk on my work pants. It doesn't matter. I'll just be stacking chairs. I finish dressing and leave. As I close the door behind me, I slide the magazine under it. Maybe, maybe the lock will hold. How late am I? I don't look at my watch. I run down the alley. The day is bright, the slush frozen. The city does not care if I am late for stacking chairs.

As I come around the corner, I see the bus pulling away. I run for it, knowing I won't make it. It doesn't matter.

The sun has come up and Peter is still dead. It occurs to me that now I have to love Jess for both of us.

I am running, running, even though the bus has already gone. When I get to the stop, I keep going. Yes, I think: Jess will make it to her audition. That's what counts today. She will light the judges on fire.

Fire.

The hot plate.

The hot plate!

I left it on!

So I turn back, I run for my life. I imagine black smoke rolling out the window. It's all my fault. My fault! But maybe I'm not too late.

We slept with it on all last night.

Around the corner, back along the alley. No smoke. Thank God! I fumble with the key, burst back in. There's the hot plate, turned off.

Cooling quickly.

Jess is standing by the bed, her jacket off, boots off.

"We left the hot plate on!" I cry.

"I'm missing my audition," she says.

"I know."

"And you're late for work."

"I know! I know!"

"I almost got to the subway," she says. "As soon as I remembered, I knew." She locks eyes with me. "It was just like when my father died. The very same feeling."

No, no. I know what she is going to say. "*Wait a minute…*"

But she keeps going. "I knew you would not remember."

"There is no fire," I say. "You feel bad because your father died, and now Peter died as well. I feel awful, too. But that's not the same as forgetting to turn off the hot plate. We *both* remembered. We *both* came back here."

She shakes her head slowly. "Too late to get to work. Too late for my audition. That's the story of you and me right there."

"Don't say that! I don't like where you're—"

"Why couldn't I say yes to you? Why not?"

"Don't ask that question!"

"Why shouldn't I?"

I try to hold her. "Because it's not too late."

"It is! It is too late." Her body is shaking.

I say, "You still have time to put on something sad and black. You can still make it to the audition. You can knock them over with the story of how your father died ... just yesterday. You can act that, can't you? And I can still make it in time to stack a million chairs."

"You want me to lie about my father?" she says.

"Not lie," I say. "Just tell a story. That's how we all get through every day. We tell stories." About Peter, about ourselves, who we are and who we love.

She hugs herself. "Is there any cereal left?" she asks.

"I finished it. I'm sorry. I will go out there and stack enough chairs to buy you all the breakfast cereal in the galaxy!" She looks so sad that I reach out and hold her. Then I run to the closet and pull out her black dress. The one she should have worn to Peter's funeral. "Put it on! Put it on! For this moment, for why the universe has plotted to bring us back together."

"Are you kidding? The only plot here is that we screwed up. I'm sorry. Last night was just ... I don't see any way forward. You're a great guy, you're really talented, you make me laugh, I love you, but—"

I try to cover her mouth. "Don't say but!"

"I *have* to say but. We have come to a certain ... a junction in our lives."

I wave the dress like a flag. "What do you mean, junction? A turning point, or a hiccup?"

"A crossroads, Gregor." I imagine her walking down some road I am somehow not allowed to follow.

"No," I say. "It's not the right word, so I'm erasing that from today, all right?"

I wipe the air with the dress as if erasing something. She locks down the corners of her mouth. Trying not to laugh.

"You can't just erase it," she says. But she's smiling. She is smiling!

I feel like I will burst from my skin. "You said 'but,' but you didn't finish. So I get to erase it. Instead, I'm going to say this. I put the snake in the box for when I was going to propose because that's how I feel about you."

"*What?*"

I have her attention. She takes the dress from me, lays it on the bed.

"It's how I feel about life with you," I say. "It could be anything. It could be diamonds…"

"I can't believe you're saying this."

"Would you let me finish?"

"You're the one who stopped me from saying *but*. I'm just—"

We stare at one another. Finally I say, "Our life together could be a diamond ring. It could be a snake jumping up in our faces. It will probably be all that and more. But it will always be interesting. And without you…"

My face feels wet. Jess pulls out a tissue.

"I don't need that," I say. I wipe my eyes on my sleeve.

"Without me, what?" she says. "Say it. You're scared."

"Of course I am," I say. "Why wouldn't I be?"

"And I'm scared without you," Jess says. "But is that a good reason to get married? Shouldn't we both go out there alone and become strong? Shouldn't we be able to stand on our own?"

"And later," I say, "when we're seventy, we can get married and whoop it up together in the old-age home."

Another smile! She cannot resist me. Despite everything. She wiggles my chin. "Seventy is the new fifty."

"That's right," I say. "And if we do our push-ups every day..."

"I've never seen you do a push-up."

I whip off my coat. "I'm starting right now!" I stretch out on the floor. "One, two, three, four." I begin to struggle. It is harder than I thought. "Five... Marry me!... six..." My arms are shaking. "Seven... Marry me!... eight... nine... ten!"

I collapse. Pathetic. Not at all how I want her to see me. I squeeze out three more push-ups, then collapse again.

"Stop!" Jess says, standing over me. "You're going to hurt yourself."

I will not give up. I will not! From the floor I groan, "Marry me!" I start another push-up, my arms burning.

"Get up!" Jess cries.

Another, up, up. *"Marry... me!"*

I collapse again. Jess rubs my shoulders while I catch my breath. "I have stacked a hundred million chairs," I say. "Why can't I do push-ups?"

"I thought you were going to hurt yourself," Jess says.

I sit up and hold my head in my hands. We are sitting close together now on the floor. But it isn't freezing, somehow. "I miss Peter," I say. "He would stop us from hurting each other. By now he'd be calling us because he was drowning somewhere. Or he was in love with some girl who didn't know he was alive. And he'd talk to you about all the mushy stuff. Then he and I would do a comedy act about the whole thing. Why didn't he just wake up?"

Jess holds me. "I know," she says.

She loves Peter. I know it. She loves us both. I wipe my eyes. And Peter loved her. And now I need to love her for both of us.

I need to do what I need to do.

"Here's the thing," I say. "Peter is dead. You have drained me. We drain each other. But—and this is the truth—you do something to the air around you. It's easier to breathe."

I look away while the words sink in. I hold out the dress again. "Are you ready?"

She looks dizzy. "What did you say?"

"You drained me."

"About the air. About breathing?" I know that smile. I know it. She looks as if she is a kid, rolling in the grass, with sunshine on her face.

"It's easier to breathe the air around you," I say. "I heard what you said in the night, when you didn't think I was there. You said that you love me and that you loved Peter. I believe Peter would want me to say those words now. About breathing. Because those words are true for me, too. And I've tried everything else."

Jess pulls on the dress. I am waiting for her to explode. But she says, "I can't lie to the Sweeney Circle judges. My father didn't just die yesterday. But I'll figure out something. And, yes."

Somehow, in the silence of our shabby apartment, my ears feel filled with music. Maybe Jess is hearing it, too. I shout, "Yes?"

"Yes!" she shouts back. "Get your coat on."

Yes what? What is she saying?

"I said, get your coat on," Jess cries. "And, about that other thing: yes!"

"Really?" I'm still not moving. "What other thing?"

The music in my head gets wilder and wilder. She suddenly looks like she wants to slap me again.

But instead we kiss: deep, long, giddy. Jess breaks it off, laughing.

"Why are you laughing?" I ask.

"Because I just said yes! And we need to go. Go!"

We both scramble to put on coats. Jess finds the ring and slips it on. It looks pretty. It looks a lot more than pretty. As we go for the door, we knock shoulders and kiss again. Then we both look at the ring.

The music in my head seems to be shaking the floor.

"But why did you say yes?" I yell. "Because of what I said? What Peter said?"

"Not now!" Jess replies. "I'll tell you in twenty years, all right? Maybe I'll understand it then. I love you. Go!"

We rush out the door. I slam it behind us. I try to lock it but now the key won't work. It doesn't matter. We run, hand in hand. Even though I'm going in the wrong direction to catch my bus. I will make sure she gets on the subway all right.

"Will the door stay shut?" Jess yells. Damn! I didn't push the magazine under it.

"Who cares?" I say, and we keep on running, straight into the wind. No gloves. No hats. But her hand is warm in mine. It's all I can think of. I can't stop smiling.

Good Reads

Discover Canada's Bestselling Authors with Good Reads Books

Good Reads authors have a special talent—
the ability to tell a great story, using clear language.

Good Reads can be purchased as eBooks, downloadable
direct to your mobile phone, eReader or computer.
Some titles are also available as audio books.

To find out more, please visit
www.GoodReadsBooks.com

The Good Reads project is supported by
ABC Life Literacy Canada.

Grass Roots Press

Good Reads Series

Bed and Breakfast

By Gail Anderson-Dargatz

Annie runs a bed and breakfast, renting rooms to overnight guests. She has lived alone since her husband died five years ago. Now, she wishes for someone to love.

One morning, Annie helps her friend Steve fix the kitchen pipes. She couldn't manage without Steve. But with his old clothes and unshaven face, he's not Mr. Right.

Then Annie hears a man's voice: "Hello?" Surprised, she bumps her head on the bottom of the kitchen sink. Jumping up, Annie welcomes Brent, her guest. Her heart skips a beat as she meets him for the first time. Handsome, charming, well dressed— will Brent turn out to be the man of her dreams?

Love You to Death

By Elizabeth Ruth

One evening, Ivy goes out for dinner with Robin and Phil, a married couple. Phil's old friend, Mark, joins them. Mark has just moved to town. He needs a place to live for a few weeks, until his condo is ready. Robin asks Ivy for a favour: can Mark stay with her?

At thirty, Ivy longs for her first real boyfriend. With Mark in her house, her wish soon gets her into trouble. But Mark has stepped into trouble, too. He has never known a woman like Ivy—and he never will again. Ivy makes sure of that.

The Clear-Out

By Deborah Ellis

Duncan is very angry. Tess, his wife, has turned their dining room into a library. For forty years, she says, she has cleaned the house while he sat in front of the TV. Now she deserves a room of her own.

Then disaster strikes: Tess gets sick, and soon Duncan is alone. Right away, he clears out the books he hates. Suddenly, things in the house start to move around by themselves. A strange message appears in the kitchen. Is the house haunted?

Scared, Duncan turns to two unlikely friends. With their help, he learns a great deal about himself, about Tess, and about lasting love.

About the Author

 Alan Cumyn began writing poetry and short stories in high school. Today, he is the award-winning author of twelve novels. His human rights novels, *Man of Bone* and *Burridge Unbound*, both won the Ottawa Book Award. Alan lives in Ottawa and teaches writing with the Vermont College of Fine Arts.

Also by Alan Cumyn:

Waiting for Li Ming

Between Families and the Sky

Man of Bone
Burridge Unbound
Losing It
The Sojourn
The Famished Lover

Novels for Children and Young Adults:

The Secret Life of Owen Skye
After Sylvia
Dear Sylvia
Tilt

*

You can visit Alan's website at
www.alancumyn.com